# A Note to Parents

*Dorling Kindersley Readers* is a compelling new program for beginning readers, designed in conjunction with leading literacy experts, including Dr. Linda Gambrell, President of the National Reading Conference and past board member of the International Reading Association.

Beautiful illustrations and superb full-color photographs combine with engaging, easy-to-read stories to offer a fresh approach to each subject in the series. Each *Dorling Kindersley Reader* is guaranteed to capture a child's interest while developing his or her reading skills, general knowledge, and love of reading.

The four levels of *Dorling Kindersley Readers* are aimed at different reading abilities, enabling you to choose the books that are exactly right for your child:

**Level 1** – Beginning to read
**Level 2** – Beginning to read alone
**Level 3** – Reading alone
**Level 4** – Proficient readers

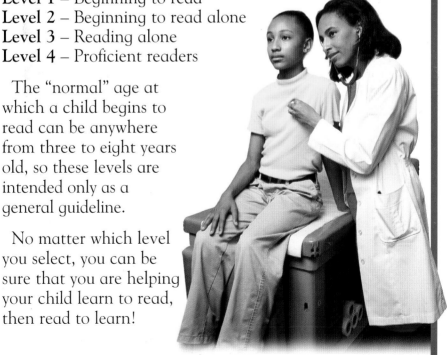

The "normal" age at which a child begins to read can be anywhere from three to eight years old, so these levels are intended only as a general guideline.

No matter which level you select, you can be sure that you are helping your child learn to read, then read to learn!

LONDON, NEW YORK, SYDNEY, DELHI, PARIS,
MUNICH, and JOHANNESBURG

Produced by Southern Lights
Custom Publishing

For DK
**Publisher**  Andrew Berkhut
**Executive Editor**  Mary Atkinson
**Art Director**  Tina Vaughan
**Photographer**  Keith Harrelson

**Reading Consultant**
Linda Gambrell, Ph.D.

First American Edition, 2001
02 03 04 05 06 10 9 8 7 6 5 4 3 2 1
Published in the United States by
DK Publishing, Inc.
95 Madison Avenue, New York, New York 10016

Published in Great Britain by Dorling Kindersley Limited.

**Library of Congress Cataloging-in-Publication Data**
Hayward, Linda.
   Jobs people do: day in the life of a doctor / by Linda Hayward.
     p. cm. -- (DK readers)
   ISBN 0-7894-7950-8 -- ISBN 0-7894-7951-6 (pbk.)
   1. Physicians--Juvenile literature.
   2. Physicians--Training of--Juvenile literature
   3. Medicine--Vocational guidance--Juvenile literature.
   [1. Physicians. 2. Occupations.] I. Title. II. Dorling Kindersley readers.

R690 .H388 2001
610.69--dc21                                    2001028427


Color reproduction by Colourscan, Singapore
Printed and bound in China by L. Rex Printing Co., Ltd.

The characters and events in this story are fictional and do not represent real persons or events.
The publisher would like to thank the following for their kind permission to reproduce their
photographs:
Key: t=top, b=bottom, l=left, r=right, c=center
**DK Picture Library:** Paul Bricknell 21; Dave King 2t; Tim Ridley 17b. **Models:** David Basilico,
Simon Basilico, Scott Fuller, Rose M. Harris, Emmitt Jackson Jr., Pena Jackson, Ariana Jackson,
Emmitt Jackson III, Zaria Jackson, Anil Jacob, David Merkle, Anna Corinne Merkle, Molly P.
Merkle, Caitlin O'Hare, Grace Segars, Jennie Segars, Ken Segars, Jeffrey Smith, Sherry Smith
and Marianne Thomas.

In addition, Dorling Kindersley would like to thank Mitzi Mize of St. Vincent's Hospital,
Birmingham, Alabama and Mary Dickinson of Pediatrics East, Birmingham, Alabama for props
and location photography.

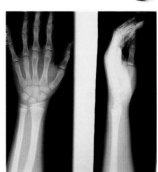

see our complete
catalog at
# www.dk.com

DK DORLING KINDERSLEY *READERS*

BEGINNING
1
TO READ

# A Day in the Life of a Doctor

Written by Linda Hayward

DK

DK Publishing, Inc.

Dr. Amy Baker
checks her pager
and makes a call.

pager

Her son, Justin, is playing
with a toy stethoscope.

"What's up?" he asks.

stethoscope

"A little girl has
a very sore stomach.
I'm going to my office early
to see her," says Amy.

"Bye, Mom," says Justin.

Amy arrives at her office.
Tim, the nurse, and
Sue, the receptionist,
are already there.

The girl with a sore stomach
has not arrived yet,
but another patient is early
for his visit.

"I hurt my finger
playing baseball,"
says Tony.

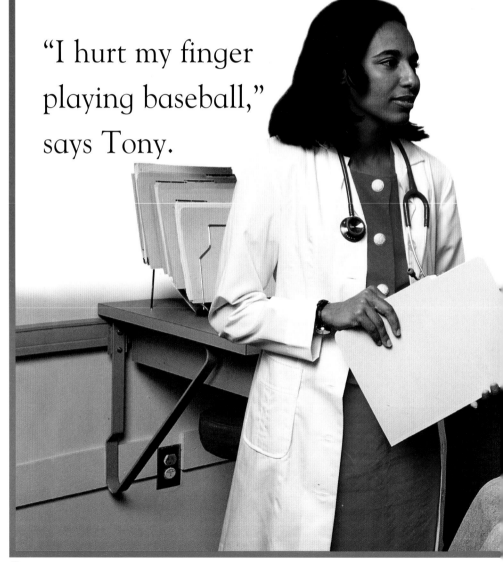

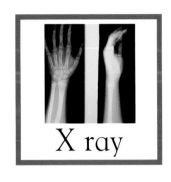

X ray

"Let's take an X ray
to make sure
it's not broken,"
says Dr. Baker.

The X ray is soon ready.
"Good news!" says Dr. Baker.
"The finger is only sprained."

She asks the nurse
to wrap Tony's finger in a splint.

splint

"The girl with a sore stomach
is here," says Sue.
"Her name is Jenny."

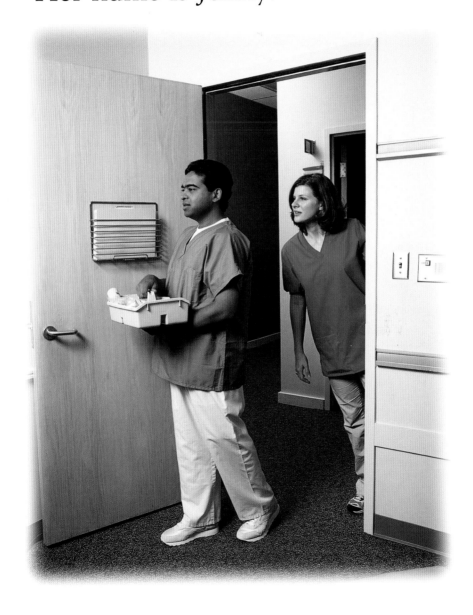

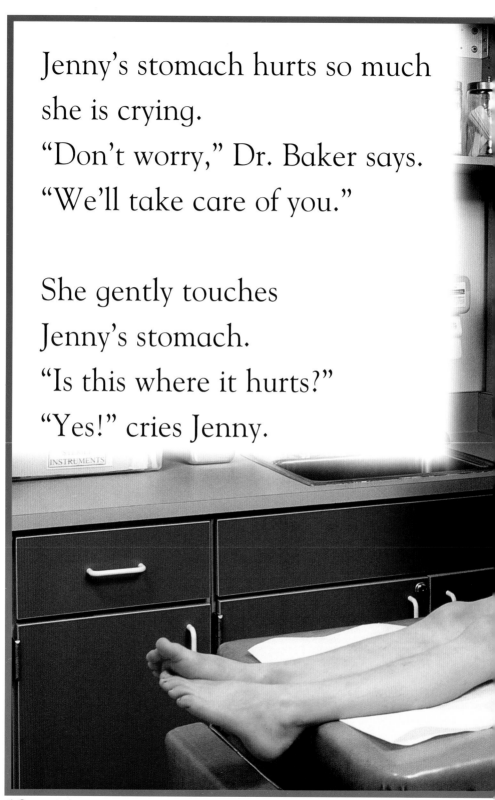

Jenny's stomach hurts so much she is crying.
"Don't worry," Dr. Baker says.
"We'll take care of you."

She gently touches Jenny's stomach.
"Is this where it hurts?"
"Yes!" cries Jenny.

INSTRUMENTS

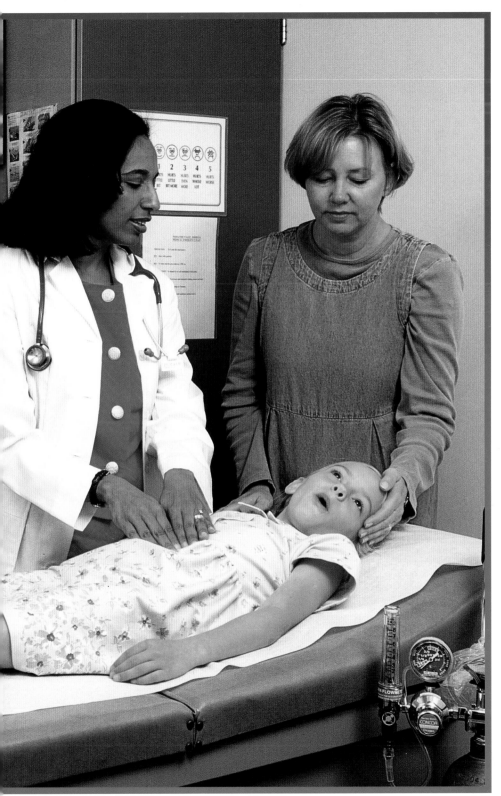

"Jenny needs an operation,"
Dr. Baker tells Jenny's mother.
"Her appendix needs to come out."

Tim calls an ambulance
to take Jenny
to the hospital.

"Dr. Baker will visit you
after your operation," says Tim.

There are more patients.
Dr. Baker uses a tongue depressor
to look at Sam's sore throat.

tongue
depressor

Dr. Baker gives Sam's father
a prescription.
"Sam needs to
take this medicine,"
she says.

medicine

Erin needs an exam to play
on her school volleyball team.
She steps on the scale,
and Tim measures
her weight and height.

scale

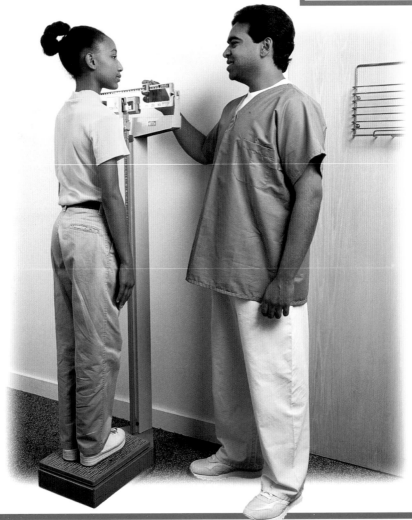

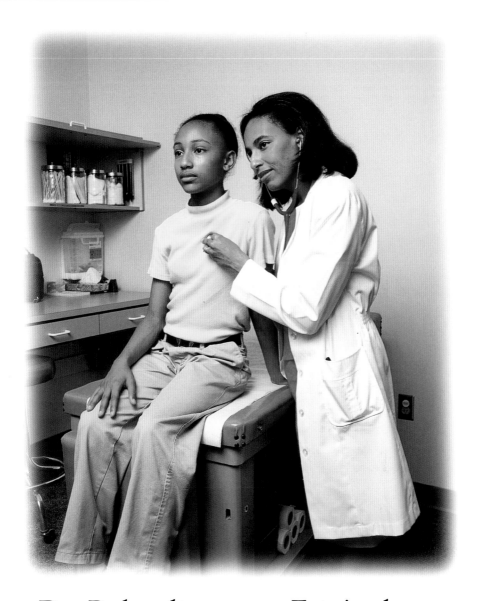

Dr. Baker listens to Erin's chest.
"Everything is fine," she says.
"You can play volleyball."

The next patient is Mrs. Taylor.
She can't stop sneezing.

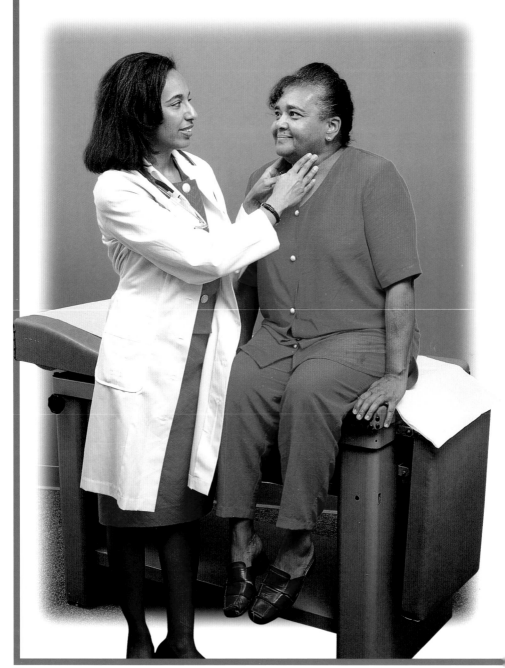

"Is there anything new
at your house?" asks Dr. Baker.

"My grandson and his cat
are visiting me," says Mrs. Taylor.

"You might be allergic
to the cat,"
says Dr. Baker.

"Sue will schedule
a test for you."

Dr. Baker also has patients
at the hospital.

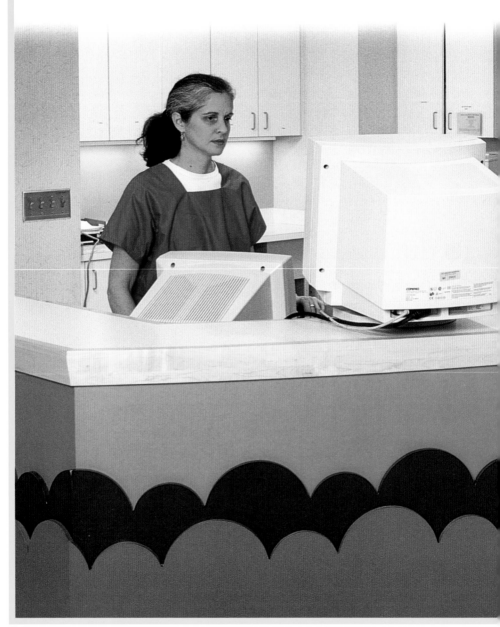

At the nurses' station,
she stops to read
her patients' medical charts.

medical
chart

Yesterday Mrs. Beale
had a baby.

Mr. Beale
has brought
her flowers.

Mrs. Beale's new baby
is Dr. Baker's newest patient.

Later Dr. Baker visits Jenny.
Her operation is over.
The doctor who took out
Jenny's appendix is there.

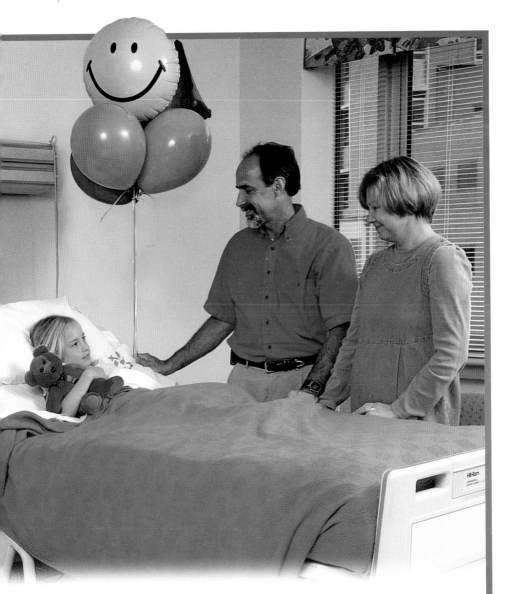

"Jenny is going to be fine,"
he says.
"She can go home
in a day or two."

Dr. Baker goes home
to her family.
After dinner, the phone rings.

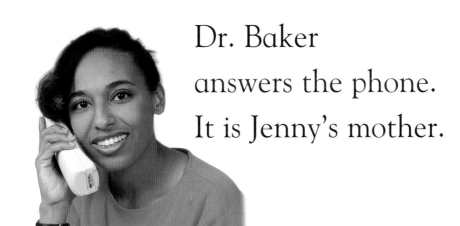

Dr. Baker
answers the phone.
It is Jenny's mother.

"We want to say thank you,"
says Jenny's mother.

"Guess what!"
adds Jenny's mother.
"Jenny wants to be a doctor
when she grows up!"

Dr. Baker smiles.
She has the best job in the world!

# Picture Word List

pager *page 4*

tongue depressor *page 16*

stethoscope *page 5*

medicine *page 17*

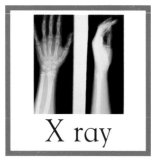

X ray *page 9*

scale *page 18*

splint *page 10*

medical chart *page 23*